P9-BBV-181

Fact Finders™

~ The American Colonies ~

# The
# Pennsylvania Colony

by Martin Hintz

Consultant:
Wayne Bodle, Assistant Professor of History
Indiana University of Pennsylvania
Indiana, Pennsylvania

Capstone
press

Mankato, Minnesota

Fact Finders is published by Capstone Press,
1710 Roe Crest Drive, North Mankato, Minnesota 56003.
www.capstonepub.com

*Library of Congress Cataloging-in-Publication Data*
Hintz, Martin.
    The Pennsylvania colony / by Martin Hintz.
    p. cm.—(Fact Finders. The American colonies)
    Includes bibliographical references and index.
    ISBN-13: 978-0-7368-2681-5 (hardcover)        ISBN-10: 0-7368-2681-5 (hardcover)
    ISBN-13: 978-0-7368-6108-3 (softcover pbk.)   ISBN-10: 0-7368-6108-4 (softcover pbk.)
    1. Pennsylvania—History—Colonial period, ca. 1600–1775—Juvenile literature.
I. Title. II. Series: American colonies (Capstone Press)
F152.H66 2006
974.8'02—dc22                                                          2004030667

Summary: An introduction to the history, government, economy, resources, and people of
    the Pennsylvania Colony. Includes maps and charts.

**Editorial Credits**
Katy Kudela, editor; Jennifer Bergstrom, set designer, illustrator, and book designer;
    Bobbi J. Dey, book designer; Kelly Garvin, photo researcher / photo editor

**Photo Credits**
Cover image: *Landing of William Penn* by Jean Leon Gerome (1863–1930), SuperStock Inc.

Capstone Press Archives/Colonial Williamsburg Foundation, 19
Corbis, 9; Bettmann, 4–5, 23, 26, 27; Francis G. Mayer, 11; Stapleton Collection, 21
Getty Images Inc./Hulton Archive, 8, 29 (left)
The Granger Collection, New York, 15, 16–17, 18
National Archives and Records Administration, 29 (right)
North Wind Picture Archives, 10
SuperStock Inc., 12–13


Printed in the United States of America in North Mankato, Minnesota.
042013
007258R

# Table of Contents

Chapter 1  Pennsylvania's First People . . . . . . . . . . . . 4

Chapter 2  Early Settlers . . . . . . . . . . . . . . . . . . . 6

Chapter 3  Colonial Life . . . . . . . . . . . . . . . . 12

Chapter 4  Work and Trade. . . . . . . . . . . . . . . . 16

Chapter 5  Community and Faith. . . . . . . . . . . . . . 20

Chapter 6  Becoming a State . . . . . . . . . . . . . . . . 24

Fast Facts . . . . . . . . . . . . . . . . . . . . . . . . . . . . . 28

Time Line . . . . . . . . . . . . . . . . . . . . . . . . . . . . 29

Glossary . . . . . . . . . . . . . . . . . . . . . . . . . . . . . 30

Internet Sites. . . . . . . . . . . . . . . . . . . . . . . . . 31

Read More . . . . . . . . . . . . . . . . . . . . . . . . . . . 31

Index . . . . . . . . . . . . . . . . . . . . . . . . . . . . . . . 32

# Chapter 1

# Pennsylvania's First People

Before European settlers came, the Lenni Lenape group of American Indians lived near the eastern coast of North America. They built their villages near the Delaware River and Delaware Bay.

The Lenni Lenape built homes of wood and bark. They lived in large longhouses during the winter months. In summer, they built round homes called wigwams. The Lenni Lenape hunted animals in the nearby forests for food. They also planted corn, squash, and beans.

The Lenni Lenape shared their land with the early settlers.

The Lenni Lenape were peaceful people. They were friendly with the European settlers who arrived in the early 1600s. The two groups got along well during the early years of settlement.

# Chapter 2

# Early Settlers

In 1609, Henry Hudson, an English explorer, sailed into Delaware Bay. When he and his men returned to Europe, they brought back maps and stories about North America. News of Hudson's trip soon brought other explorers to the area.

Around 1638, settlers from Sweden and Finland sailed to North America. They built the New Sweden colony along the Delaware River. The colony's capital was built near present-day Philadelphia.

The New Sweden colony did not last long. Dutch settlers from New York took control of New Sweden in 1655. By 1664, the English had taken the land as their own.

Settlers built the Pennsylvania Colony along the Delaware River. Pennsylvania grew to include land west of the Susquehanna River by 1763. ➡

# The Pennsylvania Colony, 1763

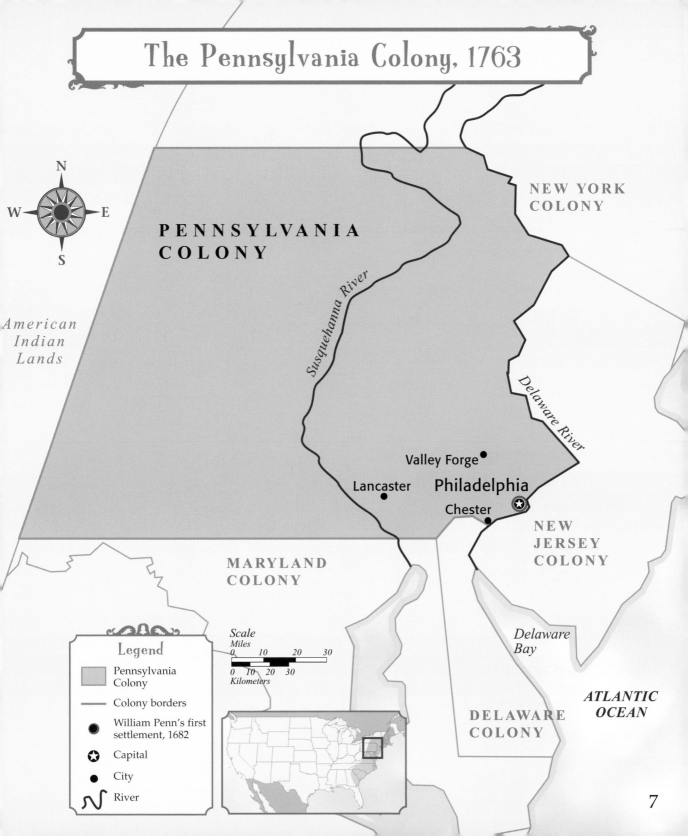

N
W · E
S

PENNSYLVANIA COLONY

NEW YORK COLONY

American Indian Lands

Susquehanna River

Delaware River

Valley Forge

Lancaster

Philadelphia

Chester

NEW JERSEY COLONY

MARYLAND COLONY

Delaware Bay

ATLANTIC OCEAN

DELAWARE COLONY

### Legend

Pennsylvania Colony

Colony borders

William Penn's first settlement, 1682

Capital

City

River

Scale
Miles
0    10    20    30
0  10  20  30
Kilometers

William Penn wanted to start a colony in North America. ⬇

## Penn's Colony

William Penn was an English **Quaker** who wanted to find a place where Quakers could worship freely. In England, the king wanted people to follow only the teachings of the Church of England. Penn wanted a colony where people could worship freely.

Penn's father had loaned a large amount of money to King Charles II of England. The elder Penn died before the bill was paid. After his father's death, Penn asked the king for land in North America to settle that debt.

▲ William Penn
received a grant
for land from
King Charles II.

In 1681, King Charles II gave Penn a **grant** for land in Pennsylvania. The king also gave him the title of **proprietor**. This title gave Penn the right to govern the colony.

Penn advertised his new colony and moved there himself in 1682. English and Dutch Quakers quickly settled on the land. Settlers could buy land for little money.

SOME

# ACCOUNT

OF THE

# PROVINCE

OF

# PENNSILVANIA

IN

# AMERICA;

Lately Granted under the Great Seal

OF

# ENGLAND

TO

## William Penn, &c.

Together with Priviledges and Powers necef-
fary to the well-governing thereof.

Made publick for the Information of fuch as are or may be
difpofed to Tranfport themfelves or Servants
into thofe Parts.

⬆ William Penn wrote booklets
to advertise his new colony in
North America.

**FACT!**

Philadelphia was one
of the largest cities in
the American colonies.

Philadelphia was the colony's first and largest settlement. Penn wanted the city to be a center of religious freedom. He named the city Philadelphia, which means "City of Brotherly Love."

## Living in Peace

Penn respected the American Indians. He formed a **treaty** of friendship with the Lenni Lenape. Penn agreed to pay the Indians for the land.

The settlers and Indians got along well while Penn was alive. When he died in 1718, Penn's sons took control of the colony.

## Stealing Land

Penn's sons did not treat the Lenni Lenape fairly. After their father's death, they claimed they found a lost treaty. They told the Lenni Lenape that the treaty gave the settlers land near the Delaware River. After stealing the Lenni Lenape's land, the Penns sold the land to settlers arriving in Pennsylvania.

Unlike his sons, William Penn treated the Lenni Lenape fairly. Penn signed a treaty to pay the Indians for their land. ▼

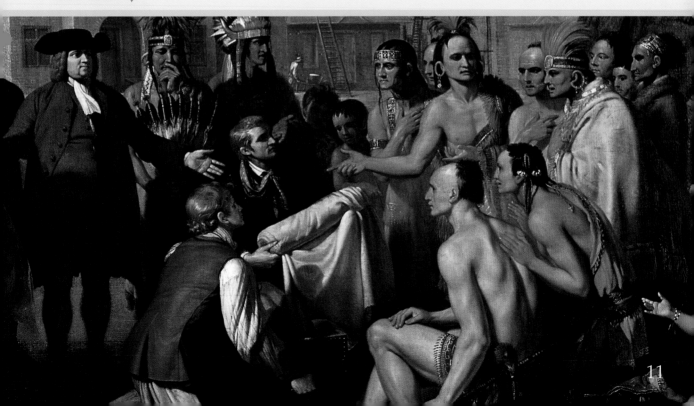

# Chapter 3

# Colonial Life

Everyone in the Pennsylvania Colony worked hard. Many boys worked with their fathers in the fields. Other boys worked for master craftsmen. They learned trades, such as shoemaking or glassblowing.

Girls worked with their mothers. They tended gardens called kitchen gardens. They used the vegetables from these gardens to feed their families. Extra vegetables were sold at market. Women also took care of cows, chickens, and other small farm animals.

Farmers grew crops to sell at market.

13

## Pennsylvania Colony's Exports

| Agricultural Exports |
|---|
| corn |
| flax seed |
| rye |
| wheat |

| Industrial Exports |
|---|
| glass |
| iron |
| rope |

| Natural Resource Export |
|---|
| lumber |

Even people in towns raised and grew their own food. Townspeople raised chickens, pigs, and cows in their backyards. They also had their own gardens.

## Education

Schools were not a large part of life in Pennsylvania. Most children did not attend school because they had to work. But colonists usually had some education. Most colonists could read the Bible and write.

▲ Quakers ran some schools in the Pennsylvania Colony. Students learned reading, writing, and math.

Quakers opened a few public schools in the Pennsylvania Colony. Students at these schools learned to read and write. Children also learned how to do simple math. Unlike some colonial schools, Quaker schools were open to all children in the colony.

# Chapter 4

# Work and Trade

Pennsylvania's first settlers were farmers. They grew wheat, corn, and rye in the colony's rich soil. Farmers sold many of these crops at markets.

As the colony grew, other businesses developed. Some colonists worked as tanners. They made shoes and other leather items. Other craftsmen made goods from iron and glass.

## Shipping Goods

Pennsylvania was one of the Middle Colonies. Its location near the Atlantic Ocean was good for business. **Merchants** could easily ship goods to other countries.

By the late 1700s, Philadelphia was a busy city.

Some indentured servants
worked for colonial craftsmen. ▼

In the 1700s, ships going
to and from England crowded
Philadelphia's port. The
shipping business made
many of the colony's
merchants rich.

## Indentured Servants

Some colonists worked
as **indentured servants**. These
servants were usually young
men and women. Indentured
servants were not paid for
their work. Instead, they
worked to cover the costs
of their trip from England to
North America. After a fixed
number of years, they were
free to start their own farms
and work at other jobs.

## Slaves

Other people in the colony also worked without pay. People from Africa were shipped as slaves to the American colonies. Some Pennsylvania colonists bought slaves to work on their farms and in their businesses. Slaves were not given a choice of jobs. They were forced to work many hours without pay.

Like the other American colonies, Pennsylvania had its own paper money. ➤

19

# Chapter 5

# Community and Faith

The Pennsylvania Colony welcomed people of many faiths. William Penn built the colony so that Quakers and others could worship freely.

The Quakers were members of a religious group called the Society of Friends. This religion began in England in the mid-1600s. Quakers met each month. They held simple religious services. Members gathered together for periods of silent prayer.

Pennsylvania's religious freedom brought other settlers to the colony. Jews, Moravians, and other religious groups found the freedom to worship that they did not have in Europe.

Quakers gathered to pray in a meetinghouse.

21

## Social Classes

Pennsylvania's colonists were divided by social class. Rich merchants were the most respected group. Professionals such as lawyers and ministers followed them. Next came skilled craftsmen, such as carriage makers and silversmiths. Laborers and servants were lower in status. Blacks were the least respected group.

## Population Growth of the Pennsylvania Colony

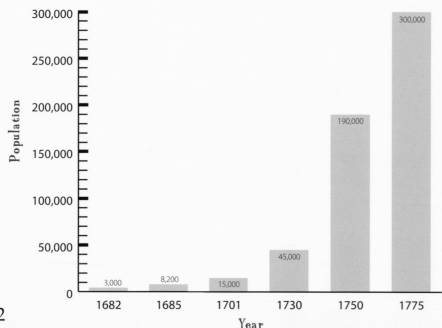

## Helping Others

Although they lived in separate classes, many colonists reached out to help others. Doctor Thomas Bond and Benjamin Franklin helped start the first hospital in Pennsylvania. Franklin also organized a fire department for the city of Philadelphia. He even helped open the first university in Pennsylvania. The work and ideas of Franklin and the other Pennsylvania colonists created a better life for many people.

↑ Famous statesman Benjamin Franklin believed in helping others. His ideas improved life for the Pennsylvania colonists.

### FACT!

Pennsylvania was the first of the 13 colonies to have a library and an insurance company.

# ~ Chapter 6 ~

# Becoming a State

As the colony's first governor, William Penn set up a government for Pennsylvania. His ideas about government were ahead of his time. He created an assembly whose members were elected. He shared governing power with the assembly. After Penn died in 1718, his basic ideas stayed in place. Penn's family continued to govern the colony until 1775.

## Troubles with Great Britain

Like other colonists, Pennsylvanians enjoyed governing themselves. They grew tired of Britain's laws. Colonists became angry with the growing number of taxes they paid to Great Britain.

Pennsylvania was one of the Middle Colonies. During the Revolutionary War (1775–1783), the colony served as a meeting place for the Continental Congress. ➡

# The Thirteen Colonies, 1763

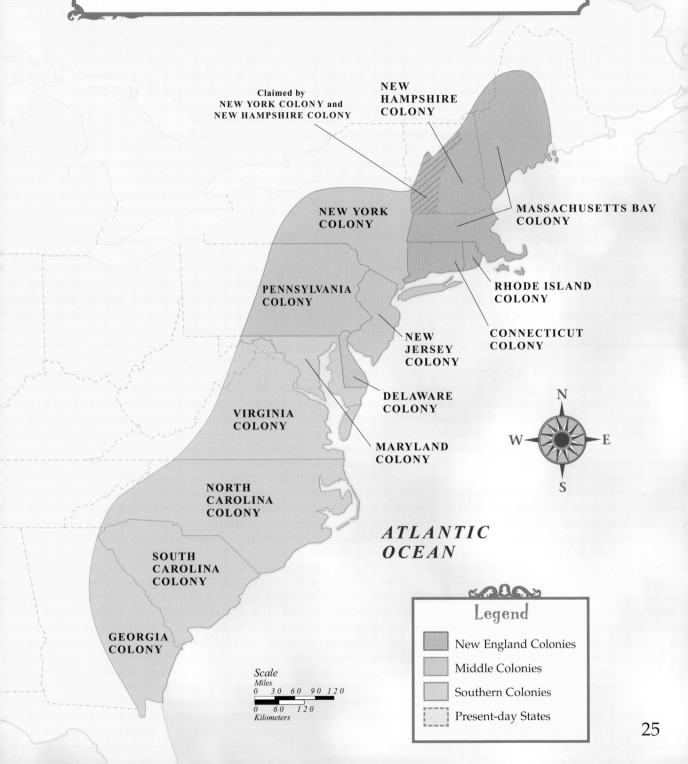

Claimed by
**NEW YORK COLONY** and
**NEW HAMPSHIRE COLONY**

**NEW HAMPSHIRE COLONY**

**NEW YORK COLONY**

**MASSACHUSETTS BAY COLONY**

**PENNSYLVANIA COLONY**

**RHODE ISLAND COLONY**

**NEW JERSEY COLONY**

**CONNECTICUT COLONY**

**DELAWARE COLONY**

**VIRGINIA COLONY**

**MARYLAND COLONY**

**NORTH CAROLINA COLONY**

*ATLANTIC OCEAN*

**SOUTH CAROLINA COLONY**

**GEORGIA COLONY**

N
W      E
S

*Scale*
Miles
0   30   60   90  120

0      60     120
Kilometers

### Legend

New England Colonies

Middle Colonies

Southern Colonies

Present-day States

25

Members of the
Continental Congress
met in Philadelphia to
sign the Declaration
of Independence.

Troubles with Great Britain continued to grow. In April 1775, the Revolutionary War (1775–1783) began. The colonies fought Britain for their independence.

In July 1776, representatives from the colonies approved the Declaration of Independence. This document declared the colonies free of British rule. But Great Britain did not accept the declaration.

Pennsylvania played an important role in the war. In the winter of 1777–1778, General George Washington housed his troops at Valley Forge in Pennsylvania. The American troops eventually went on to defeat the British.

In 1787, leaders from the former colonies met in Philadelphia. They wrote a framework of laws called the **Constitution** of the United States. On December 12, 1787, Pennsylvania adopted the U.S. Constitution. It became the second state to join the United States.

**FACT!**

Representatives met in Philadelphia to sign the Declaration of Independence. Today, the city is known as the birthplace of America.

General George Washington and his troops spent a winter at Valley Forge, Pennsylvania. ▼

# Fast Facts

## Name
The Pennsylvania Colony (named for William Penn's father)

## Location
Middle colonies

## Year of Founding
1682

## First Settlement
Philadelphia

## Colony's Founder
William Penn

## Religious Faiths
Amish, Catholic, Church of England, Jewish, Lutheran, Moravian, Presbyterian, Quaker

## Agricultural Products
Flax seed, rye, wheat

## Major Industries
Iron, lumber, manufacturing

## Population in 1775
300,000 people

## Statehood
December 12, 1787 (2nd state)

# Time Line

**1681**
King Charles II of England gives William Penn a land grant.

**1707**
An Act of Union unites England, Wales, and Scotland; they become the Kingdom of Great Britain.

**1777-1778**
General George Washington houses his troops at Valley Forge.

**1783**
America wins the Revolutionary War.

**1682**
William Penn and a group of settlers come to Pennsylvania.

**1763**
Proclamation of 1763 sets colonial borders and provides land for American Indians.

**1776**
Declaration of Independence is approved in July.

**1638**
Settlers from Sweden and Finland settle New Sweden.

**1609**
English explorer Henry Hudson sails into Delaware Bay.

**1775**
American colonies begin the fight for independence from Great Britain in the Revolutionary War.

**1787**
On December 12, Pennsylvania is the second state to join the United States.

29

# Glossary

**constitution** (kon-stuh-TOO-shuhn)—the written system of laws in a state or country that state the rights of the people and the powers of the government

**grant** (GRANT)—a gift such as land or money given for a particular purpose

**indentured servant** (in-DEN-churd SUR-vuhnt)—someone who agrees to work for another person for a certain length of time in exchange for travel expenses, food, or housing

**merchant** (MUR-chuhnt)—a person who buys or sells things for profit

**proprietor** (proh-PREYE-uh-ter)—a person given ownership of a colony

**Quaker** (KWAY-kur)—a member of the Religious Society of Friends, a religious group founded in the 1600s that prefers simple religious services and opposes war

**treaty** (TREE-tee)—an official agreement between two or more groups or countries

# Internet Sites

FactHound offers a safe, fun way to find Internet sites related to this book. All of the sites on FactHound have been researched by our staff.

**Here's how:**

1. Visit *www.facthound.com*
2. Type in this special code **0736826815** for age-appropriate sites. Or enter a search word related to this book for a more general search.
3. Click on the **Fetch It** button.

**FactHound will fetch the best sites for you!**

# Read More

**Catrow, David.** *We the Kids: The Preamble to the Constitution.* New York: Dial Books for Young Readers, 2002.

**Fingeroth, Danny.** *Democracy's Signature: Benjamin Franklin and the Declaration of Independence.* New York: Rosen, 2004.

**Williams, Jean Kinney.** *The Pennsylvania Colony.* Our Thirteen Colonies. Chanhassen, Minn.: Child's World, 2004.

# Index

agriculture. See farming
American Indians. See Lenni Lenape

capital. See Philadelphia
Charles II, King (of England), 8, 9
children, 12, 14, 15
Continental Congress, 24, 26
crops, 13, 14, 16, 28

Declaration of Independence, 26, 27
Delaware Bay, 4, 6
Delaware River, 4, 6, 11

education. See schools
England. See Great Britain
exports, 14

farming, 4, 12, 13, 16
first settlement. See Philadelphia
Franklin, Benjamin, 23

Great Britain, 8, 18, 20, 24, 26

Hudson, Henry, 6

indentured servants, 18
industries, 14, 16, 28

Lenni Lenape, 4–5, 10, 11

maps, 7, 25
markets, 12, 13, 16, 18

New Sweden, 6

Penn, William, 8–10, 11, 20, 24, 28
  father, 8, 28
  sons, 10, 11
Philadelphia, 6, 10, 17, 18, 23, 26,
  27, 28
population, 22, 28

religions, 8, 10, 20, 28
  Quakers, 8, 9, 15, 20, 21, 28
Revolutionary War, 24, 26, 27

schools, 14–15
shipping, 16, 18
slaves, 19
statehood, 27, 28

taxes, 24
treaties, 10, 11

U.S. Constitution, 27

Valley Forge, 27

Washington, George, 27